100 M

for

Writing for

Film

and

Television

http://www.facebook.com/pages/SCRIPT-
DOCTOR/138062651688?ref=ts

978-1-4461-9401-0

Introduction

For those of you haven't read this book's predecessor, I suppose my initial question would be 'What are you playing at? Does the word 'More' in the title not give you a clue? Go buy the first one, you mooncalf'.

But not for the first time in my life (nor indeed in the last hour) I'd be wrong, and not just in using archaic insults for pretension's sake. You can read this book first, or the last one. You can open it at page 23 on each copy and go backwards through one book and forwards through the other – it makes no difference.

I should explain I don't really like textbooks and I especially don't like textbooks that have the audacity to 'tell' you, point by point, how to write the perfect drama. Ignoring the fact that, while a few come close there's no such thing as the perfect drama, there is certainly no magic formula that will produce a hit screenplay.

That doesn't mean that there aren't a thousand different techniques, strategies and rules you can apply to hugely improve your writing, it's just that if you try and follow a set recipe, you'll pretty much end up with a cake that's already been baked a thousand times and that everyone's sick of eating.

So for those of you haven't bought the first book yet, consider this volume somewhere between a series of flashcards and a Tarot deck. Dip into it at moments when the mind is blocked, or leave it lying around in your writer's inner sanctum to idly flick through.

Those who *have* bought the first book already know that this series of tips was created on a whim for a Facebook page I set up in 2009; the first tip was posted and soon after a colleague made a wager with me that I couldn't produce a tip for every weekday for a year. I won that wager and accidentally published a book out of it. By necessity the tips had to fit the character-limitation of a facebook post, and through personal preference I decided not to plan it in any way, to simply come up with a fresh tip pretty much off the top of my head, based on my long years of writing TV drama.

So don't look for any structure, don't look for magic bullets, philosopher's stones or holy grails. And if you haven't bought the first book, I say again 'What are you playing at?'

SCRIPT DOCTOR, SEPTEMBER 2010

Unless your central character is a sociopath or a substance abuser, you should avoid them making random spontaneous decisions; let's see the turning points, inspirations and motivations that force your protagonist to act (subtly, of course).

Beware trends. Just because a slew of genre movies/books/TV are popular now, it doesn't mean that's what the networks are looking for. Developing a project can take years so a current trend is aging from the moment you start typing. If you want to write something commercial, try and predict the trend to come; save yourself the heartache and toil of development hell.

A common oversight. Big news should touch every character it affects. All too often we only see the protagonist's reaction to the big event and the minor characters carry on as normal. Convey the complexity of the aftermath by the differing responses of your cast.

Scripts are slippery creatures; when you read back your first draft it will almost certainly have wriggled off in an unexpected direction. Make the choice to rein it in and get it back on track, or take a leap of faith and follow it down a new path. Don't try and do both at the same time, for that way madness lies.

Don't let things drop in your protagonist's lap. If it's information, have them figure it out or work to get it. If it's money or love, have them earn it. Even if its just getting from A to B make it a challenge. Not only is it simply better drama, nobody likes a hero who seems privileged or lucky.

Looking for examples of tight, seat-gripping plotting to improve your own narrative skills? You could do worse than check out the kids section, whether it be film or books. Children don't fall for post-modernism, pastiche or symbolism, they want story, event and character. Roald Dahl, Pixar, Alan Garner, Pullman, Alcott – it's an endless list. Learn from the master story-tellers.

Dialogue howler: 'Something like that' as a guarded response, as in 'So what was it? Bad break-up/Parental issues/Sibling rivalry/Unfortunate spelunking incident?'... 'Something like that'. Tired and over-used. Replace it, but not with any sentence that starts 'Let's just say....'.

While you should generally strive to segue effortlessly from scene to scene with verbal and visual links, sometimes a harsh, abrasive cut can be used to disorient the viewer and put them on edge.

Adaptations. Film and TV have a totally different language to prose and theatre. If you're considering an adaptation, think outside the original text and structure. Theatre often looks slow and static on screen while the linear and massively detailed nature of prose often makes it impossible to be faithful to the original. Be bold and ruthless with your re-working.

What kind of sick puppy are you? Can you confront your beloved protagonist with grotesque adulteries that tear their heart from their chest? Can you maim and kill? Can you wreak hellish injustice on the innocent? Can you devise cruel and horrendous emotional and physical tortures? If the answer is an immediate no, you may want to reconsider being a writer.

Curing your unconscious plagiarism is best treated like stop-frame animation. If you or a reader has identified a scene or plot element as being familiar from another source, but you need the sense of that scene, rewrite it several times. Make a small change to dialogue, setting or action on each draft. Seven drafts or so in, it should be unrecognisable and wholly yours.

Not so much a dialogue howler, as a curiosity. The most commonly used line in English language cinema? 'Let's get out of here'... and while it never really seems to jar, I can't help but feel we should be looking for alternatives.

Who's minding the baby? It's often tempting when your central characters are off-screen to have someone in the scene explain where they are and why they're not there. It's very rarely necessary.

Regardless of their importance in the action, the characters you should expend the most effort on are the ones furthest removed from yourself; the opposite sex, the most distant by age, the ones with whom you share the least in common. If you surround a well drawn solid hero with cardboard cutouts your script will fail.

'Let's start at the very beginning, it's a very good place to start'. Or is it? The natural inclination is to tell your story in a linear chronology, but look at it again after a couple of drafts. Is there anything to be gained by starting at the end? Or in the middle?

What are your opening scenes trying to achieve? If you're throwing the audience straight into the action or dialogue be sure you can maintain the pace and intrigue till you come to a natural rest stop. If you're going for slow establishers presenting your 'world', make damn sure they're interesting and have a purpose.

Dialogue - the Verbal Tic. Starting lines with 'well', 'look', 'hey', 'right' etc. It seems to be some sort of nervy habit, like a little throat clearing before writing the actual dialogue. Or maybe we think it makes the dialogue sound more like speech - it doesn't. Mercifully, thanks to good editors, these rarely make it to the screen, but take them out of your script at every draft. They're just messy.

If you're cutting away from a scene mid-conversation and planning on returning to it, you need to find a natural interruption. If you're away from the scene for more than a few seconds and you come back to it at the same point you left off, it just looks as if the characters have been waiting for you to come back.

It's usually a good rule-of-thumb never to report off-screen action but it's a rule that's often worth breaking, especially for comic effect. Sometimes a moment of high farce that might come across as too slapsticky or childish on screen can be far funnier when recounted after the event with the perfect choice of words.

How thick is your skin? Can you take a tidal wave of criticism and objectively decide which is accurate and which is misplaced? This business is tough, tough, tough on the ego. Be confident about your work, but be ready to recognise and accept good advice when it's offered.

Are you employing a voice-over narrative? If so, why? Does it add a complex narrative layer? Is it establishing your work as genre-homage? Is it manipulating the audience into believing one thing before sucker-punching them with a twist? In short, have you got a bloody good reason for it or are you just short-cutting to avoid finding a better way of telling your story visually?

A stage direction howler; the over-use of the word 'suddenly'. Unless an action is gradual, then it's pretty much certain to happen 'suddenly'. Using the word 'suddenly' is usually redundant, especially if 'suddenly' applied to an action which isn't particularly surprising. Also, as you can see, it quickly becomes redundant and loses its impact.

If you want to see the rules of dramatic seeding laid bare, check out a really good farce. You can learn a lot about the normally hidden mechanics of set up and pay off - like taking the back off a watch to see the workings.

What are your characters doing the first time we see them? What does it tell us about who they are? And more to the point, is it interesting to watch - does it inform and intrigue?

You're writing a screenplay/script, not directing a movie or show. Unless they're absolutely necessary to explain an effect, leave out the instructions for fancy camera angles, whip pans and smash cuts. They break up the reading experience. Remember your script has to be read before it can be filmed.

Your central character is not you - it's really tempting to cast a wittier, smarter, sexier version of yourself in the lead role in your drama, but do that and you'll lose your objectivity and judgement.

Practical advice - always proof your work on hard copy, not on the screen. You get a better sense of how it will be read and it gives you a chance to read your work through thoroughly a couple of times.

Good dialogue is not about writing the way people really talk. Good dialogue is about making well-chosen, communicative, interesting language sound like real conversation.

When you're in deep on a single project day after day, try to steer clear of other people's work that may connect with your script's content. It will inevitably bleed into your work. Plus there's nothing more annoying than wrestling with that big plot point all day, solving it, then turning on the TV to see some other joker got there first.

If you're planning a major shift in geographic location deep into your final acts, consider its effect. Will it jar on the audience and damage the carefully constructed ambience? Or will it prove a welcome relief and symbolise a sudden shift in emotional status of your characters?

Bad subtext is almost worse than writing 'on the nose'. Too often writers use 'knowing' subtext, where one character is deliberately and consciously masking their intent. In true subtext the characters unwittingly reveal themselves through otherwise innocent dialogue and action.

Relationships constantly change, growing or failing in small increments, rarely in major events. If you're aiming for a semblance of reality, manufacture and show those minor but all-important turning points.

Is your work station slowing you down? The quality of your chair is probably more important than the quality of your laptop; dodgy posture is going to make you tired quicker and fill less pages.

Realism is over-rated and almost impossible to achieve. Strive for an internal, solid model of reality that functions as its own world. Make the audience believe.

Are you as visually literate as you think you are? HBO, Kaufman and Gondry are all well and good but cast your net through time and space too. There's almost a century of movies, over half those years of TV drama and English is not the only language. Cast your net wide and learn from the enduring masters.

How do we know what your central character's thinking and planning? The sidekick/best buddy's not just there for light relief; they're your audience's 'in' to the workings of the protagonist. Use them wisely.

In a screenplay, action is language, and just like dialogue, has developed its own cliches. Beware the framed photo, the smashed whiskey glass, the spooky musical box and all their ilk.

All drama is, in essence, detective fiction, with the audience as detective. Even in a romance or broad comedy, you have to offer mysteries and lay clues to their solution.

I can pretty much guarantee you're over-writing your dialogue. We all do it, but we don't all know we're doing it. Even if every line is a corking gem, if your characters' conversation isn't actually getting them anywhere, make some cuts.

Shady characters rarely speak or behave shiftily; they're usually business-like matter-of-fact or cocky. Are you being true to character or just telegraphing the audience of your intent in a cheap and easy shorthand?

Just because people work or live together doesn't mean we only need to see them in the office or at home. Liven up the visual and give yourself options for movement and interaction by taking them out of their usual environments.

If you're looking for a way to cut your dialogue down to its bare essentials, check out a few of the better graphic novels. They're great for demonstrating how to trim conversation down to take up minimum space and cover periods of prolonged action while still maintaining a natural flow.

It's great that you feel compelled to write that well-researched story of human injustice and social conscience, but simply cataloguing the miseries and tribulations of an individual or group does not make drama; the same rules apply as they do to any other script. Nothing kills your message quicker than the stink of 'worthiness'.

Sounds stupid, but you'd be surprised how often people miss this. Give your script a cover page with a date, the title and your name and contact details; and make sure it has page numbers. Personally I also like a header or footer with the title and author too for those rogue pages that go adrift. If a reader loved your script and it's in a pile with 120 others, how will they find it again?

Don't let your big final action sequences step on your plot revelations. Important plot points will either slow up the flow or get lost in the rush.

Sometimes it's good to get into the undergrowth. If you're worrying about one of your smaller through-lines, cut and paste all of its scenes into a separate document and work on it as though it was a short film, then slot the scenes back into their original locations.

Every script has its own narrative language; decide after first draft what language your script is using. Throwing in filmic devices willy-nilly to shortcut through story is like suddenly writing a single scene in Cantonese.

When the big emotional turning point hits your character it's tempting to have them react right away. Sometimes it's more realistic to store that response away for a while; we all know this delay works well in acts of vengeance, but it can work for positive emotional turning points too.

Avoid the temptation to give 'ouchy' dialogue to characters in pain. It seems to be a strange compulsion we have to verbalise these moments, but I'm sorry, a graphic description of someone getting shot in the thigh and falling to the ground spouting claret is only diminished when followed by something like 'Ow, my leg!'

Are you writing a small drama set amidst a much larger cataclysm? If so, be mindful of that scale; a well-written, low-key personal story can complement and focus the themes of the bigger picture but a badly-written one will simply lose the audience's attention in comparison to the greater horrors.

I know it's hard to chose your title, but try not to pick one from a line of your dialogue. It always jars on the ear and can break the fourth wall by reminding you you're watching a work of fiction.

Take comfort that even the best writers don't always know what they're doing when they start a big series. As an experiment, watch the final episode of the last season of your favourite box set then the first episode of season one back to back.

What's your moral compass? Your script doesn't have to have a message, but you must consider the ethical code of your characters. It doesn't have to be an admirable system, it can even be totally amoral, but it must be thought through and it must be either consistent, or changed through experience.

Don't use dialogue to highlight the cunning metaphors and ironies of your plot. An emotionless villain with a heart condition could be clever symbolism. Having a character make reference to it is over-egging the pudding.

The devil is in the detail and thus is the heart of subtext. Take a look at that blazing row you've just written for the cuckolded husband, or the heroine coping waiting for those cancer test results. Now try writing it again but make the dialogue about the burning of the toast, forgetting to buy detergent or a long forgotten song on the radio. Better, isn't it?

Research is not confined to books; it's life experience too, either your own or second-hand from others. You'd be surprised how easy it is to access people from all walks of life, background, profession and life-experience. Most organisations have some sort of community liaison facility - give them a call. Talk to people.

Make your pitch document draw them in. Don't go straight into a mass of text. Go for a cover page with just the title, contacts details, logline and format, then a second page with one of two short paragraphs of broad overview before you start hitting them with the in-depth stuff. Keep your plot synopsis to two pages or less.

Don't plaster your script and covering materials with 'copyright' notices and intellectual property warnings. It's vaguely insulting and largely unnecessary. Plagiarism by production companies is almost non-existent. Telling your ideas to other writers is a different matter - we are unscrupulous thieves.

That lover's tiff that slowly builds to screaming fever pitch is best NOT ended with a passionate kiss. Too predictable.

Beware over-compensating when writing the opposite sex. Bad enough to conform to gender stereotypes, but almost as bad to go too far in the other direction and lose those elements of gender difference that are true without being cliches.

While accidental repetition in dialogue must be carefully sought and deleted, deliberate repetition of key phrases can be very effective either as a comic device or to instil a sense of menace.

Tragedy is not bad things happening to people. Tragedy is bad things happening to people as a result of their own fatal flaw, or even better, as a result of a well-meant but ill-considered act. It isn't enough simply to heap misery on a character, there has to be a dramatic cause and effect.

Predictability is never a good thing, but you can use a sense of inevitability - the knowledge that events or characters are being drawn inexorably to a crisis - to power your script's motor.

In 'straight' drama, your central character usually needs certain strengths and pro-active qualities. In comedy you can relax this a little and allow your supporting cast to play 'large' at the central character's expense (as long as there's a turning point where your hero eventually grasps the nettle).

Take joy, pleasure and pride in your work, but don't be precious about the job itself; keep perspective. We're essentially crazy people sitting around half-dressed making things up; bear that in mind when you're writing characters with 'real' jobs and treat them with respect.

You've got a lot to say about a lot of things but you don't have to say them all at once in the same place. That kid's fantasy story you're writing may not be the best place to discuss the Stalinist post-war pogroms AND coming of age bisexuality. Take it easy; there'll be other scripts and stories.

Yes you need a strong first scene, but no-one ever wrote an opening line that sold their work from the off. Stop killing yourself and concentrate on the next 100 pages.

On the screen your script will need establishing shots and post-action breathing spaces. Don't worry too much about including these on the page, keep the pace flowing - rhythm and space can be saved for the shooting script and the edit. Hook the reader for now.

Writing phone calls is a nightmare. Don't just bash them down cutting from one talking head to the other (if for no other reason than that it eats up page-space). Think about reaction shots and movement and getting the best dramatically from both. Best of all, unless the use of the phone is in itself a vital part of the plot, avoid it in the first place.

Don't 'fantasy-cast' in your script. It's fine to imagine that all-star cast in your head, but on the page it's far better to let the reader use their own interpretation. Not to mention the slim, but not unprecedented occasion of an actor getting hold of a draft and finding another thesp's name all over it.

I'm constantly hearing people saying they'd write that first great screenplay 'if they only had the time'. Can you fill a page in an hour? Or half an hour? Of course you can - so you could have a first draft in around three short months.

Self censorship; if you don't believe art can have a negative impact, then surely you can't think it capable of exerting a positive influence. In which case why are you bothering to write at all? Think about the message you're putting across.

Writing comedy on your own can be like trying to tickle yourself. Get a buddy who shares a similar (but god forbid not identical) sense of humour. Work on those gags and polish them hard.

You wouldn't write a character with a medical condition without doing your research first, so why do the same with a psychiatric illness or learning difficulty? It's not just that it's sloppy writing - learning the pathology of a condition helps you set rules that will lead to better plot turns.

Great comedy dialogue is not writing gags for characters to say out loud. It's about cadence, rhythm, vocabulary and character shining through the lines; it's about understatement and overstatement and the marriage of the two. Great comedy dialogue flows like music, gags are a stop/start staccato.

Flesh out those minor characters to give them a little more depth and interest, especially in comedy. Try the 'adjective/noun' game. A list of adjectives on one page and professions, hobbies, nationalities etc on the other. Thus your bland pizza delivery boy, waitress, shop assistant etc becomes 'nervous angler', 'hirsute plumber' or 'belligerent Icelander'.

An accent or a funny voice does NOT give a character depth or comedic potential. The people of Belfast, Barnsley and Birmingham don't walk around all day thinking how hilarious everyone sounds and old ladies don't talk in high croaky voices. If you wouldn't do it with a black, Asian or Jewish character, don't do it.

Where will it end? If you think your opening scene's a tough one, the final scene presents problems of its own. It's hard to finish right on the climax, so what will you choose for your aftermath scene? Keep it short, make it visually interesting and if at all possible, avoid dialogue. It's really hard not to sound glib.

.

Do you need to lose weight? Your script feels the right length and you've made every word count but it still comes in at 140 pages. Go through your lovely elaborate stage directions and fancy scene cuts and hack mercilessly. Most readers will be taking your script home; don't make them carry a brick.

How's your backbone? You think all those rejections are hard? Wait till you get an acceptance or a regular gig. For all the lip service paid to the writers' importance, we are often seen as an unavoidable inconvenience and with a few wonderful exceptions, loyalty is an alien concept and professional courtesy just as remote. Can you handle it?

Technology affects narrative. Just as edit technology changed the format of filmic story-telling, so today computer gaming is opening up new structures. Learn the classic forms for sure, but be aware that changes are already happening in the way your future audience perceives narrative.

Can you pitch your script in 25 words or less? Try an exercise - pick ten of your favourite movies and see if you can totally encapsulate them inside the word-limit (without using the poster byline).

You're in the early stages of piecing together a story based around a major event, possibly a true story. The natural urge is to build to the climax, but try something different and open with your event and follow the aftermath; see where it takes you.

A good thriller taps into people's desires to have their expectation subverted while trying to outguess you. At first draft write each act as if it really is going the way everyone expects it to go, even if that means that the acts don't necessarily hang together yet. When the pages are full THEN you can start throwing in the clever stuff, the twists and ties that make it work.

Always Avoid Alliteration - nice in poetry, clumsy in prose, you need to watch for it accidentally occurring in dialogue, but especially don't give characters alliterative names unless you're playing it for laughs. Stan Lee has a lot to answer for, and trust me, with my name I know this to be true.

Make your turning points clear but not obvious; it's an insult to your audience, and more importantly your characters, to have them suddenly reverse a lifelong opinion or state-of-play after a single incident that contradicts their world view. Be subtle, be smart, be true.

Learning's a wonderful thing; the courses, the books and the tips are invaluable, but writing is one of the few vocations where it's best to try and forget all the rules while you're actually doing it. Try to write instinctively and save the rules for the editing process.

John Donne got it right; 'any man's death diminishes' or at least it can damage your script if you treat death too lightly. A plot-serving death without a genuine emotional reaction or response strips the humanity from your script.

Enjoy your first draft, no matter how hard it feels. It's the only time you get to take the long way round to your destination. The cul de sacs can be frustrating but on the way you'll get to see some beautiful scenery that you might want to revisit on a different trip. Every subsequent draft will be spent making your journey shorter and more familiar till by draft six, you're virtually a commuter.

The personal IS political. The rule of 'show don't tell' has even more meaning in political drama. Diatribes, factual rants, hectoring lectures and polemics are usually off-putting. Make your point and spread your message through action, emotion and event and let the viewers draw their own conclusions.

Stuck? Uninspired? You may not know it but one of your most invaluable resources is close at hand. Dig out all your old notebooks and spend a couple of hours flicking through. You might be surprised by what chimes with your current project.

Script Notes; the more the merrier. Some people panic at the sight of pages of notes on their work, but it's often a good sign. Fine tweaks need many notes, it only takes a paragraph to explain that a script's never going to work, so don't panic if a briefing seems to take forever. Take clear notes and be reassured that it's a sign you're almost there.

Ironically, even a flashback must drive a plot forward. The placement of a flashback is just as important as its content. Does your flashback reveal information that your subtext has already made clear? If so lose it.

You can learn a lot just from the physical hard copy presence of your script. Watching it come off the printer or a simple flick-book style lookthrough before you read can reveal great swathes of dialogue or stage directions, twelve page single scenes or single pages of twelve scenes that you may miss on a proper read if you're engrossed in your own brilliance. Try it.

Does your villains' plan make sense or is it just there to provide you with twists and turns? Whether it's a couple of pickpockets or a coup d'etat, real villains don't come up with elaborate and convoluted schemes just to give their enemies clues.

A brilliant idea is like a new lover - stay in with it all day, have fun, do beautiful and terrible things to each other in private - but be aware that once you show it to friends and colleagues it may turn out you've been making the same mistake you have with every previous relationship.

Elegant, stylised, Deadwood-esque soliloquising or clearly-insane-rambling aside, your characters really shouldn't talk to themselves; especially not if stressing that key moment of realisation of a vital plot point.

Don't attribute your cultural references. We're a smart sophisticated audience, we don't need to be told where your quote comes from; just throw it in with the assumption that if both well-loved characters get it, so will the audience.

Are you asking too much with your stage directions? Does your hero enter the room 'with the air of a man troubled by childhood trauma, yet secretly pleased at his recent encounter with a would-be lover'? Stop it.

Learn the rules. Then Break Them All.